UN DARE TO BE COMMON

MEN'S BIBLE STUDY

TONY DUNGY

Group

Loveland, Colorado

group.com

Group resources actually work!

This Group resource incorporates our R.E.A.L. approach to ministry. It reinforces a growing friendship with Jesus, encourages long-term learning, and results in life transformation, because it's

Relational
Learner-to-learner interaction enhances learning and builds Christian friendships.

Experiential
What learners experience through discussion and action sticks with them up to 9 times longer than what they simply hear or read.

Applicable
The aim of Christian education is to equip learners to be both hearers and doers of God's Word.

Learner-based
Learners understand and retain more when the learning process takes into consideration how they learn best.

DISCOVERING HOW TO IMPACT YOUR WORLD

Visit our website: **group.com**

Credits
Contributors: Tony Dungy and Karl Leuthauser
Editor: Carl Simmons
Executive Editor: Becki Manni
Copy Editor: Zach Carlson
Chief Creative Officer: Joani Schultz
Art Director: Paul Povolni
Book and Cover Designer: Jean Bruns
Production Manager: Peggy Naylor

Unless otherwise indicated, all Scripture quotations are taken from the *Holy Bible*, New Living Translation, copyright © 1996, 2004. Used by permission of Tyndale House Publishers, Inc., Carol Stream, IL 60188. All rights reserved.

Scripture quotations marked "NIV" are taken from the HOLY BIBLE, NEW INTERNATIONAL VERSION®. Copyright © 1973, 1978, 1984 by International Bible Society. Used by permission of Zondervan Publishing House. All rights reserved.

ISBN 978-0-7644-3920-9
10 9 8 7 6 5 4 3   18 17 16 15 14 13 12 11 10
Printed in the United States of America.

CONTENTS

n *uncommon* life doesn't happen by accident. It's the result of the choices, actions, and commitments we make—to God, to ourselves, and to others.

It's not all about big commitments, however. God uses the dozens of little commitments we make every day to prepare us for the big ones. When we choose to live them out in God's strength rather than our own, we grow. What we do in practice, we'll do in the real game.

So let's kick off our practice time together. You'll help each other train together as we examine what's critical to living an uncommon life. And as you do that, you'll discover how to impact your world in ways you haven't yet imagined.

In Session 1, we'll work on strengthening your core. Why aren't more men prepared to live an uncommon life? How can you live out that life even when it's not popular or easy? We'll look at the roles we already play in life, how our successes and our failures reveal where we're at right now, and how to move forward from here.

The first place an uncommon life plays out is in the home, and that's what Session 2 is all about. Our actions speak louder than our words. We'll examine how our actions affect the rest of our family, for good and bad, and how to invite God into changing our actions when we need to.

In Session 3, we'll work on lifting up our friends and others we know. It's easy to let other commitments get in the way of our friendships. It's uncommon to put our friends first. How can others around us get built up as we follow Jesus' example? How can we be a friend to others? And how can we find the friends *we* need? We'll look at all of that together in this session.

Every man asks himself, "What am I going to do with my life? How can I make a difference?" Here's something every man needs to understand: We make an uncommon difference when we say yes to God and allow him to guide our steps. So we'll discover what God's built us for—and how to keep our focus—in "Session 4: Your Full Potential."

Again, it's God's desire to give meaning and purpose to each of our lives. But we always need to remember that it's *God's* meaning and *God's* purpose. In "Session 5: A Mission That Matters" you'll discover what it will take for us to make room for God's plans.

In Session 6, we'll take a closer look at the "platforms" God's already given each of us—the places and situations where God's put us—and how we can best use them. Every day we're fed messages, expectations, and images that push us to live a life other than the one God has planned for us. We'll examine those messages and what we can do to counteract them.

We'll close this study by remembering what our foundation for an uncommon life is: our relationship with Jesus. What are we really putting our faith in? If it's anything but Jesus, it's a false hope. When we make Jesus the guiding force of our lives, we can't help but live an uncommon life.

God has given each of you dreams and goals that only you can fulfill. There are always risks in stepping out and doing the things God's put on your heart right now. But it is always worth it. It's my prayer that this study will give you the encouragement and some fresh new ways to begin following those dreams.

So begin walking those dreams, together. Dare to be *uncommon.*

—TONY DUNGY

Tony Dungy made a decision to live his life with *Quiet Strength,* the way God intended. And millions of football fans and non-football fans alike have seen the results of that by Tony's *Uncommon* actions and character both on and off the field.

In January 2009, God gave Tony's life another dramatic turn. At age 53, Coach Dungy chose to walk away from a 31-year NFL career—one which took him from player, to the first black coach to win a Super Bowl ring—so that he could take the next step forward in pursuing the uncommon life God's prepared for him.

With this study, Tony invites *you* to *Dare to Be Uncommon*—to discover your life's mission and live it out to the fullest. And that big mission starts with little steps.

Thus, the issues you'll explore in this study are issues men wrestle with throughout their lives. How do I maintain my character, in *all* parts of my life? Who can help me move forward, and how can I help them back? How can my life have significance, even after I'm gone? Let Coach Dungy be *your* coach as you walk together through these and more questions over the next seven weeks.

This study is meant to be done in a group setting, whether it's a men's breakfast on Saturday morning, a small group meeting in a home, a restaurant, or church, or even as a lunch group at work. Everyone who participates will gain a deeper understanding of how they can impact their world—your world.

You'll want everyone to get a copy of this study, so they can work through it both during and between meeting times. Make sure you also get the DVD that accompanies this study, so all of you can hear Coach Dungy's pep talk for each week and get ready to go out and make these principles real in your lives. We recommend that each participant get a copy of Tony Dungy's book *Uncommon* as well.

Briefly, here's how the sessions break down.

Think About It

You'll spend time thinking about the session's topic. A simple experience will ease you into the topic and help you start thinking about it. Then you'll talk about the connections between the experience you just had and your own life experience.

Talk About It

In this section you'll take things a little deeper. The discussion here will tie your life connections to the Bible passages in the next section. This is an important time to get to know what's on other guys' minds and hearts and to help each other walk through the things you discover together.

Study It

This section is where you'll dig into the Bible and see the principles you discover exemplified in God's Word. Through further discussion and sharing, you'll connect your earlier discussions and experiences to the discoveries you make in different passages.

Live It

This brings the study full circle. Just as you started the session by reflecting on your life, you'll have a chance to reflect again, this time connecting to your life what you've taken from the study. The activities will guide you in making these connections.

Commit to It

Before you conclude your session, it's important to commit to an action point that will help you continue to grow. We'll give you four options to choose from.

STRENGTHENING YOUR CORE

DEVELOPING UNCOMMON CHARACTER INSIDE AND OUT

WHAT EACH PERSON WILL NEED:

- Bible
- Pen
- Camera or camera phone

Think About It

Without any conscious direction from you, your body knows how to take care of itself. If you were facing hypothermia, your body would let fingers, toes, and other extremities go before it let your vital organs die. If you were starving or dehydrated, your body would do whatever it took to keep those core organs working–to keep you alive as long as possible. Your body knows that damage or loss of your core leads to irreparable or even deadly consequences.

Pass your books around the room, and have each person write his name, phone number, and e-mail address in the space provided on pages 71-72 of this book.

When you see this icon, have someone in your group read the section aloud as everyone else follows along.

Your spiritual health and life aren't that different. Damage or compromise of your spiritual core can also lead to irreparable or deadly consequences. To live an uncommon life, you must protect and build your core. And in order to do that, you need to understand what your core is–who you *really* are.

9

Let's begin this study by thinking through what our core really is, so we're ready to move forward from here. For each of the sentences below, choose the one word you think best describes you. You might think of several words you can put in each space, but try to narrow it down to one word that really captures who you are. Some possible answers follow each sentence.

I most value _____

(friendship, honesty, faith, integrity, wisdom, laughter, hard work, family, relationship, money, God's Word, fun, freedom, success)

I strive hardest for _____

(growth, knowing God, peace, advancement, love, understanding, self-improvement, obedience, reaching my potential, glorifying God)

I will never _____

_____

(abandon my…, turn away from…, quit, cheat, lie, forget…, leave…, steal, fail to…, stop…)

If your group is still getting to know each other, have everyone share their completed core statements with the rest of the group. This will help group members understand where others are coming from very quickly.

Find a partner, and share your answers. Discuss why you chose the words you did for each sentence.

 UNcommon TRIVIA *Morgan Wootten was inducted into the Basketball Hall of Fame in 2000. What significant fact about Coach Wootten's career sets him apart from other basketball Hall of Fame coaches?*

Talk About It

"Integrity is that internal compass and rudder that directs you to where you know you should go when everything around you is pulling you in a different direction."

COACH DUNGY

 At the professional sports level, players are so specialized that few of them ever change positions. There *are* exceptions—sometimes a tight end moves to the interior line, or a receiver joins the defense. Sometimes a lineman has even played the role of running back. But the longer an athlete stays in and practices a position, the more likely he or she is to stay there. The routine of the position helps develop the skills the athlete needs to play well at that position.

Likewise, every man has a number of roles or positions he fills. Some of us are students. Most of us work. Some are fathers, and all are sons. The longer we stay in a role, the more it shapes—and even defines—who we are.

Every role we fill provides tremendous opportunities to grow and develop. But every role also provides challenges to our core. Your role in your job or school can distract you from putting Jesus first or being available to your family. Your role as a father or son can tempt you to take loved ones for granted. We sometimes can substitute serving in ministry for serving Jesus.

Think about the major roles you've had in life and how they've helped shape who you've become. Maybe your sales job has taught you how to close a deal. Maybe your studies have nudged you toward either becoming high-strung or becoming a slacker. Perhaps fatherhood has deepened your wisdom or sense of responsibility.

For each of the roles below, think how that role has helped make you who you are today and how it might provide a challenge to your core. An example is included to get you started.

AREA	ROLE	HOW IT HAS SHAPED MY CORE VALUES	HOW IT CAN CHALLENGE MY CORE
Family	Fatherhood	Challenges my selfishness	Desire to provide causes me to focus too much on money and advancement.
Career/ School			
Family 1 (Son, Father, Brother, etc.)			
Family 2			
Volunteer Work/ Ministry			
Other			

Discuss:

▶ *What's the greatest challenge to your core that you're currently facing?*

▶ *How will you be true to who you are in the midst of that challenge?*

Which two men in the Bible claimed their wives were actually their sisters? Hint: Like father, like son.

Study It

 Everyone has flashes of goodness and great moments. But a man's core is measured by his consistency. A man of character and integrity remains true to his core in difficulties, regardless of the possible outcome. Jesus showed special interest and concern for a person's core and consistency. Let's look at two examples that show Jesus' value for consistency.

Form groups of four. With your group read Matthew 23:23-27 and John 8:3-11, and then discuss:

▶ *What differences do you see between the woman and the teachers of the law?*

▶ *Why do you think Jesus' reactions to the teachers of the law and the woman were so different? How would you have reacted?*

▶ *Do you relate more to the teachers of the law or the woman caught in sin? Explain.*

Live It

"Ultimately, character and its growth don't come from rules but from small actions of responsibility that occur day after day."

COACH DUNGY

 The teachers of the law presented themselves as complete, knowledgeable, and close to God. In fact, they were proud, religious, misguided, and far from God. The woman caught in adultery, on the other hand, could do nothing but lean on Jesus' mercy. To find character and core issues in your life, start by looking at how the way you present yourself fits with what's really going on inside.

Have everyone who has a camera on his phone (or another digital camera with him) raise it in the air. Form groups of three or four, making certain every group has at least one camera.

Take a picture of each person in your group. Have each person look at his own photo for 20 seconds. While you look at your photo, think about this one question only:

▶ *How do you present yourself to those around you?*

Now write your thoughts to this question here:

Now think about what's going on inside you. Make special note of the things that don't quite fit with the image you try to present to others. For example, you may want your boss to think you're a loyal employee. But if you're honest with yourself, you find that you often throw him or her under the bus when talking to fellow co-workers.

With a partner, discuss:

▶ *What problem in your core character do you think God is pointing out to you?*

▶ *How do you think that problem got started? How can it be fixed?*

If you have the *Dare to Be Uncommon* DVD, watch the first segment together as a group. Discuss:

▶ *What choices are you facing right now? What decisions would best reflect your core character, and what will it take to see those decisions through?*

Commit to It

Before you conclude this session, commit to one or two of the action points that follow or another you come up with. Be prepared to share what happened or what you learned next week.

Option 1: Read Part I, "Develop Your Core," and Part II, "Love Your Family," in Coach Dungy's book *Uncommon*. When you see an area where God's calling you to a higher level of core living, underline it and pray about it.

Option 2: Old habits die hard, so get help changing a problem with your core or character. Ask one of the other guys in your group to be an accountability partner, who can ask you how it's going in this specific area of your life every week until this study is complete (and hopefully beyond!).

Option 3: One big problem with our character flaws is that we're often blind to them. Take a step that requires courage: Ask someone who really knows you, like your spouse or parent, to help you identify one or two of your major character flaws. Don't defend yourself; listen to your friend or family member, and thank that person for his or her honesty.

Option 4: We're responsible for making the right choices, but real change to who we are comes from beyond our own strength and will. If God's revealed something wrong with your character or core, ask for God's help. Use these steps:

1. Apologize to God for the specific actions or attitudes that have come out of this character flaw.

2. Determine to go in a different direction, continually asking God for strength and help to move forward.

3. Remove yourself from media or situations that reinforce or feed the flaw.

4. Ask a friend, relative, pastor, or counselor for help and accountability with this issue. Serious character flaws are often a result of serious pain or trauma. Ask a pastor or Christian counselor to help you work through the root of the issue as you continually move through steps 1 to 3.

LOVING OUR FAMILIES

THE UNCOMMON POWER OF PUTTING OTHERS FIRST

WHAT EACH PERSON WILL NEED:

- Bible
- Pen

Think About It

 No man in his right mind sets out to hurt the ones he loves. But we all have seen, experienced, and maybe even lived through it. A man can wreak havoc on his family through the wrong focus, thoughtlessness, the inability to hold his tongue or temper, or simple selfishness.

When you see this icon, have someone in your group read the section aloud as everyone else follows along.

Think about how each of the following common choices men make affects those they love. For example, when a father hastily calls his child a name such as "weak," "stupid," or "incompetent," the child might take that term on as part of his or her identity for the rest of his or her life. With a partner, think about possible results for each of the following actions. Pay special attention to the effects these actions have on others.

17

1. When a man focuses too much on work, his wife or children might…

2. When a son doesn't respect his parents, they might…

3. When a father expects too much of his child, his child might…

4. When a husband spends too much time watching TV or surfing the web, his wife might…

5. When a father is overbearing with his family, it might…

6. When a father is too passive, his family might…

With your partner, discuss:

▶ *Share one positive and one negative example of how your father has made a lasting impact on your life.*

▶ *What's one thing you do that may be negatively impacting your family? How else might it affect your family if you continue doing it?*

Talk About It

"Love means being active in the life of your family."

CoACH DuNGY

 Like it or not, your words and actions have tremendous power. Some men don't understand that power and misuse it out of pain or ignorance. Others are paralyzed and overwhelmed by it. Many new fathers are terrified that they're going to disappoint or damage their sons or daughters. Too many fathers of teenagers believe they've already failed. Some sons believe they've created a relational chasm with their parents that can't be crossed.

The good news is that it's never too late to start being a good dad or a loving son. Even if you've failed your family multiple times, there's always hope for restoration and relationship. You have incredible power and opportunity to be a God-honoring positive force in the lives of your family members.

You've already thought through how our selfish actions affect those we love. Now, think about how each of the following simple *positive* actions can have a long-term effect on the people you love. Get back with your partner, and think about possible results for each of the following actions.

1. When a man spends time with his family on a regular basis and is truly focused on *them*, his wife or children might...

2. When a son makes a real effort to consistently work around the house and serve his family, his parents might...

3. When a father is quick and consistent to apologize for the mistakes he makes, his children might...

4. When a husband regularly works at serving and loving his wife, she might...

With your partner, discuss:

▶ *What's one thing you intentionally do that has a positive impact on your family?*

▶ *What kind of long-term impact could that action or behavior have on your family members?*

▶ *What would you like to start doing with or for your family that you have a hard time doing right now?*

 Who holds the NFL record for the most career fumbles?

Study It

"But don't just listen to God's word. You must do what it says. Otherwise, you are only fooling yourselves."

JAMES 1:22

 Imagine that you worked for a boss who seemed to like your work. But imagine that this boss never really told you he was happy with what you did. In fact, you never received a raise, heard or received any encouragement, or saw any semblance of advancement. Over the years, you began to doubt if your

boss even knew you existed. Finally, you decided to throw in the towel. When you told your boss why, he was shocked that you didn't know how much he appreciated you.

We all love our families. But we need to act on and openly express that love. Love without action does as much good for your family as a boss's appreciation without expression. Love, as it's defined in Scripture, has very little to do with feelings. The Bible shows that love is much more concerned with choices and actions than feelings and emotions.

First Corinthians 13 shows us what love is all about. It's not a list of what love *feels* like. Rather, it is a list of what love *does*. If you want to know whether you really love your family, consider how you're living out 1 Corinthians 13.

Read 1 Corinthians 13:4-7. Then complete the survey on the next page based on how you are living out love toward your family.

Form groups of three or four. Have each person share his two strongest and weakest areas of love. Then discuss:

▶ *What specific actions do you think you'll take, based on what you just discovered?*

▶ *What changes do you think will occur with others* because *of those changes?*

UNCOMMON EVENT

Whom did Jesus ask, "Do you love me?" and how many times did he repeat the question?

I am patient with my family:

1	2	3	4	5	6	7	8	9	10
NEVER				SOMETIMES				ALWAYS	

I am kind toward my family:

1	2	3	4	5	6	7	8	9	10
NEVER				SOMETIMES				ALWAYS	

I avoid envy and jealousy with my family:

1	2	3	4	5	6	7	8	9	10
NEVER				SOMETIMES				ALWAYS	

I avoid pride (and boasting) with my family:

1	2	3	4	5	6	7	8	9	10
NEVER				SOMETIMES				ALWAYS	

I am not rude with my family:

1	2	3	4	5	6	7	8	9	10
NEVER				SOMETIMES				ALWAYS	

I am not self-seeking with my family:

1	2	3	4	5	6	7	8	9	10
NEVER				SOMETIMES				ALWAYS	

I am not easily angered with my family:

1	2	3	4	5	6	7	8	9	10
NEVER				SOMETIMES				ALWAYS	

I walk in forgiveness of my family:

1	2	3	4	5	6	7	8	9	10
NEVER				SOMETIMES				ALWAYS	

I protect my family:

1	2	3	4	5	6	7	8	9	10
NEVER				SOMETIMES				ALWAYS	

I trust and hope for the best with my family:

1	2	3	4	5	6	7	8	9	10
NEVER				SOMETIMES				ALWAYS	

I persevere with my family:

1	2	3	4	5	6	7	8	9	10
NEVER				SOMETIMES				ALWAYS	

Live It

"I know not all of you are fathers, but to those of you who are, I have one request: Be there for your children!"

COACH DUNGY

 We've all make big mistakes with our families. Fortunately, 1 Peter 4:8 tells us that "love covers a multitude of sins." The first step to really loving your family is being truly *with* them. More than your provision, instruction, security, and strength, your family needs *you*. The greatest evidence of your love is your presence.

If you want to be truly present with the members of your family, join them in the things *they* love and appreciate. Your wife may not fully appreciate your presence while you watch a football game together, but she may feel incredibly connected with you if you ask her to go on a walk.

Pick two members of your immediate family who need to see your love in action. For each member, list what he or she likes, and think about how you can connect with that family member by doing those things with him or her.

Family member name:_____

His or her interests:_____

How I'll connect: _____

Family member name:_____

His or her interests:_____

How I'll connect: _____

With a partner, discuss:

▶ *What changes do you hope to see with the family members you just listed as you connect with them more?*

▶ *What kind of "ripple effect" might it have with other members of your family?*

DVD ▶ If you have the *Dare to Be Uncommon* DVD, watch the second segment together as a group, and then discuss the following question:

▶ *How can you follow Coach Dungy's encouragement to put your family first?*

Commit to It

Before you conclude this session, commit to one or two of the action points that follow or another you come up with. Be prepared to share what happened or what you learned next week.

Option 1: Read Part III, "Lift Your Friends and Others," in *Uncommon.* When you see a passage that impacts an area of your life, underline it and pray about it.

Option 2: Make a plan to take at least one member of your family on an unforgettable experience. Plan a camping trip, a drive to the Grand Canyon, a ride in a limousine, or a night at a concert or play. Put it on your calendar now, and make it happen.

Option 3: When a man makes a mistake with a family member, he often tries to make it up to him or her by buying something or doing some "nice" thing. Here's something even better you can do: Repent. First, apologize. Second, turn away from that action or behavior. If there's a mistake you've made that's hurt a family member, make it up to him or her—*God's* way.

Option 4: When Coach Dungy began working for the Kansas City Chiefs, he realized he had to find a way to make time for his family. So he gave up golf. Is there something you need to give up so you can really be there for your family? Can you trade off one of your hobbies for one you can do with a family member? Can you give up a TV show, project, or pastime to make more time for your family? Either find a way to bring a family member into your activity, or let it go for a season.

LIFTING YOUR FRIENDS AND OTHERS

BECOMING AN UNCOMMON FRIEND AND BROTHER

WHAT EACH PERSON WILL NEED:

- Bible
- Pen

Think About It

"Life was meant to be lived in community."

COACH DUNGY

 Chris has 178 friends on Facebook. Between managing his Facebook, MySpace, fantasy football, instant messaging, and text messages, he'd have a full-time job if he could figure out how to get paid for it. He knows a lot of people, but at the end of the day, Chris would tell you that he actually feels like he's kind of on his own.

Mike has a freshman son and a boy in middle school. Facebook and MySpace arrived a little late for Mike. Besides, between work, keeping up on house projects, and driving his kids around town, who has time for friends? If he had time to think about it, Mike would probably enjoy hanging out with the guys. But his family is close, and he's doing what he needs to do to keep things running.

The Bible clearly shows us that God wants us to have meaningful friendships and even tells us the kind of friends we need: "A man of many companions may come to ruin, but there is a friend who sticks closer than a brother" (Proverbs 18:24, NIV). When it comes to friends, Scripture indicates that quality is much more important than quantity. Let's try something that may shed some light on this truth.

Introduce yourselves to one another. Yes, again. But you're going to do it a little differently this week. Find someone you don't know well, and take 30 seconds each to share one outstanding example of commitment you know about. Go!

After a minute has passed, say:

Find another person you don't know that well, and take *another* 30 seconds apiece to share about an official commitment *you've* made—to a job or a team, for example—and how that commitment changed over time.

Again, allow only a minute for pairs to share.

OK, one more: Find one more person, and share about the longest commitment you've made to another person, such as a marriage or a friendship. This time, take a minute each to share how that commitment has changed *you* over time.

After two more minutes, have everyone sit down. Discuss the following questions:

▶ *What was enjoyable about this activity? What wasn't so enjoyable?*

▶ *How was this "meet and greet" time like some (or more than some) of the relationships you have right now?*

▶ *Let's revisit the last question you discussed in your pairs. How did the person you talked about become your friend? What happened to take it to the next level?*

Talk About It

 Let's take another look at the second half of Proverbs 18:24: "But there is a friend who sticks closer than a brother." A quality friend sticks by you in tough times. A real friend makes life better. A real friend makes a real difference in your life. Distance doesn't diminish the support. Time only strengthens the bond. No matter what you have done or what's happened, you can always count on a quality friend.

One way to do a quick assessment of your current friendships is to think about whom you'd turn to in various situations. Write down the name of the friend (excluding your spouse or other family members) who you'd call if:

1. You needed a ride to the hospital or someone to watch your kids while you took your spouse or child to the hospital at 2:00 a.m.

2. You got fired from your job.

3. You were getting sued for a decision you made at work, or you caused a fatal car accident.

4. You fell into a sin that could change the rest of your life.

Discuss the following questions with three or four others:

▶ *What do your answers reveal about the current status of your friendships?*

▶ *What does it take—or what do you think it would take—to find a friend who sticks closer than a brother?*

Study It

"Don't relish conflict, but don't fear it."

COACH DUNGY

 Proverbs 18:24 was likely written by Solomon. As king, Solomon surrounded himself with hundreds of wives and concubines. Unfortunately, his many companions led to his ruin. Solomon's father, however, had one of the most remarkable friendships in the Bible. Is it possible that Solomon was comparing his own experience to that of his father, David, when he wrote the proverb? Whatever Solomon was thinking about, the words he wrote serve as a tremendous guide for us some 3,000 years later. And the example David gave his son deserves our study and consideration.

In groups of three or four, read 1 Samuel 20:1-42. Then discuss:

▶ *Talk about a time when a friend made a sacrifice for you.*

▶ *What price did Jonathan pay to remain loyal to David? Why do you think he was willing to pay that price?*

▶ *What other characteristics can you identify in David and Jonathan's friendship? What would it take to build these attributes into the friendships you already have?*

 UNCOMMON
EVENT   *Which of Gideon's sons killed 70 of his brothers at once?*

Live It

"Too often, we evaluate a friendship based on the way it benefits us. But lasting friendships are formed when we can cause those benefits to flow toward someone else."

COACH DUNGY

 You may have a friend like Jonathan. If not, you probably want one. When it comes to creating deep friendships, there's a simple truth that can guide you: If you want a friend, *be* a friend. If you're looking for a friend who's loyal, be loyal to your friends. If you're looking for a friend who'll reach out to

you, refuse to give up on reaching out to your friends. Over time, your faithfulness to others will develop faithful friendships. Your friends don't have to be just like you. They don't have to share all the same interests. But if you find a friend who's following after God and is a man of character, be his friend.

God is likely calling you to grow deeper in a friendship or to start a friendship. Before you begin, consider the following:

▶ *Think about a person you believe God may be calling you to become friends with, or a friend you think God may be calling you to go deeper with. Write his name here:*

▶ *What sort of friend are you to that person right now? How can you be a better friend?*

▶ *What are you looking for in a friend? How can you help bring those characteristics out in your friend?*

DVD ▶ If you have the *Dare to Be Uncommon* DVD, watch the third segment together as a group, and then discuss the following question:

▶ *What can you do in response to Coach Dungy's encouragement to be an uncommon friend?*

Commit to It

Before you conclude this session, commit to one or two of the action points that follow or another you come up with. Be prepared to share what happened or what you learned next week.

Option 1: Read Part IV of *Uncommon*, "Your Full Potential." When you see an area where God's calling you to realize your full potential, underline it, pray about it...then act on it!

Option 2: Whose name did you just write down during Live It? Invite him to do something fun with you or with you and your family. Put dates in your calendar *today* for the next four months to remind you to reach out to that friend at least twice per month. You can even jump-start a friendship by inviting your friend into an unforgettable adventure. Plan a backpacking trip, a day of bungee jumping, a mission trip, or a family skiing trip. Adrenaline, challenge, and shared goals are catalysts for building friends.

Option 3: It shouldn't come as a surprise that some of the deepest, longest-lasting Christian friendships come out of small groups with other men. Identify another man who God may be leading you to connect with—he might be going through this study with you. Ask him to become a prayer partner or accountability partner, and meet at least twice per month. Go through a book together, share what God's doing in your lives, or just pray together. But make it a long-term commitment.

Option 4: Read your Bible, and study examples of friendship there. David and Jonathan provide one tremendous example of friendship in Scripture. Consider also studying Ruth and Naomi's friendship in Ruth 1–3, Elijah and Elisha's friendship in 2 Kings 2:1-18, and the fellowship of the early church in Acts 2:42-47. You can dig even deeper by studying Proverbs 17:17; 27:10; 27:17; Ecclesiastes 4:9-10; and John 15:13-14.

YOUR FULL POTENTIAL

MAKING AN UNCOMMON DIFFERENCE IN GOD'S KINGDOM

WHAT EACH PERSON WILL NEED:
■ Bible
■ Pen

Think About It

"Seek the Kingdom of God above all else, and live righteously, and he will give you everything you need."

MATTHEW 6:33

 When most men think about their potential, they often think in terms of their careers. When you look at the men who reached their potential in Scripture, though, it's interesting to note that we seldom hear about their success at work. We never hear about Paul's excellence in making tents. Moses never became a sheep-herding mogul. Peter didn't work his way up to a fleet of fishing boats.

These men found their potential in loving God with all their hearts and in striving to advance God's kingdom with all their might. Paul brought the good news to the Gentile world— while making tents on the side. Moses found his potential when he followed God's command to confront the Pharaoh of

Egypt. Peter reached his potential as he nurtured and led the early church.

How would our lives—even our world—be different if we, like these men, understood that our true potential is realized in our focus on advancing God's kingdom? Your full kingdom potential is found somewhere in the intersection of the opportunities God has given you, the talents and abilities God has entrusted you with, and the passions God has put in your heart.

"Ultimately, it's not really a career question. It's a purpose question. What am I going to do with my life?"

COACH DUNGY

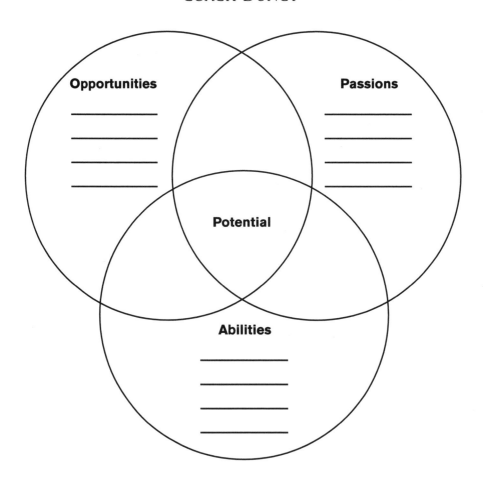

As you work through the following exercise, set aside your aspirations for your career or education and focus on your kingdom potential. In the left circle of the diagram, write down a few opportunities where God has already used you for the kingdom and one opportunity you think may be before you right now. For example, you could list "shared my faith with my neighbor," "taught a Bible study," or "could help a co-worker make the right choice."

In the bottom circle, list a few of the strengths and abilities God's given you—for example leadership, problem solving, encouragement, or determination.

In the right circle, list a few of your passions and things you care most about. Again, try to focus on passions that are connected with God's kingdom. For example, you could list healthy marriages, outreach, worship, or freedom.

Once you're done, look over your diagram and look for ways that all three of these areas are (or could be) connected in your life. Can you see a common thread or focus? Can you identify an area or focus in God's kingdom where you have potential to make a difference? In the middle portion where the three circles converge, write a word or two that describes the way you can make a difference. For example, you could write "teaching couples," "mentoring friends," or "leading an outreach."

 *Some guys who reach their potential just happen to be at the right place at the right time. Which NFL quarterback threw a pass that was so lucky it became known as the "Immaculate Reception"? Bonus question: Who caught it?*

Talk About It

> *"Focus on those things that you want to occur, not those that you do not want to occur."*

COACH DUNGY

 If there was ever an area where we should dream big, it's the impact God wants us to make for his kingdom. There is so

much to gain and so little to lose when we chase after the things of God with all our hearts. God can use you to change a life, start a ministry, or change a community. But sometimes we have a tough time seeing the potential we have. Sometimes we need others who believe in us before we'll start moving toward that potential.

Write your name in the space below. Get in a circle with four other guys and pass your book to the guy immediately to your right. Prayerfully consider the potential you see in the person whose book you're currently holding. Write down what you see in that person and what you believe he has the potential to do for God's kingdom. One example is done for you. Then pass the book to the next person on the right. Spend about one minute with each book prayerfully considering the person, and continue the process until you have your own book back.

Name: _____

WHAT I SEE IN YOU...	I BELIEVE YOU HAVE THE POTENTIAL TO...
A desire to know the truth	*Teach others who have big questions about Christianity*

With a partner, discuss the following questions:

▶ *Compare what you wrote in the middle section of your Venn diagram with what others wrote about you today. Do you see common thoughts or themes? What did others point out that you* hadn't *seen in yourself before?*

▶ *What items in your list above resonate with you? Explain. What would it look like if you applied your passions and abilities to those opportunities?*

Study It

 What prophetess in the Bible was afflicted with leprosy, and what did she do wrong?

 Moses is certainly one of the top five men in history when it comes to living up to kingdom potential. Leading a group of slaves out of the most powerful empire on earth and across the Red Sea, delivering the Ten Commandments, and writing the first five books of the Bible all seem like accomplishments of a man who met his potential.

But it's important to remember that it took a *long* time before Moses reached his potential. He was 80 years old when he first confronted Pharaoh. There were a number of things Moses had to work through to reach his potential. Let's take a look at some of the things that Moses had to overcome.

In groups of four, read each of the following passages. For each passage, discuss the following questions:

▶ *What did Moses need to work through in these verses?*

▶ *How does (or might) a similar issue affect your own potential?*

1. Exodus 2:11-15

2. Exodus 4:10-13

3. Exodus 5:4-21

4. Exodus 14:1-14

Live It

> *"You won't always rise to the level of the expectations you have for yourself, but you will never be able to rise above the imaginary ceiling you construct in your mind."*
>
> ———
> COACH DUNGY

 Not even Moses' own fears and mistakes stopped him from reaching his potential. God's plan for Moses was bigger than Moses' human frailty and mistakes. Here's Moses' secret, and the one thing that every man in the Bible who reached his

potential did: He ultimately said yes to God. Even though he was afraid, Moses went back to Egypt. Even though he couldn't speak well, he stood before Pharaoh. Even though he wasn't sure what to do, Moses held his hand out over the Red Sea as God parted it in two. Moses shows us that reaching our full potential isn't as much about doing the right things as it is about doing things with the right heart.

▶ *Think about a time when you first said no to what you thought God wanted you to do, but then ultimately said yes. Share your story with a partner.*

▶ *What did God teach you as a result of your obedience?*

Now think about one to three things you think God may be asking you to do. Write them down here:

With your partner, discuss:
▶ *How can saying yes to each of these things help you reach your potential?*

▶ *What keeps you from consistently saying yes? What (or who) could help you get past those obstacles?*

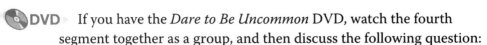 **DVD** If you have the *Dare to Be Uncommon* DVD, watch the fourth
segment together as a group, and then discuss the following question:

> ▶ *How can you stay focused on your God-given goals and what God*
> *wants your life to become—rather than focusing on what your life* **isn't**
> *yet?*

Commit to It

Before you conclude this session, commit to one or two of the action
points that follow or another you come up with. Be prepared to share
what happened or what you learned next week.

Option 1: Read Part V of *Uncommon*, "Establish a Mission That
Matters." When you see an area where God's speaking to you about your
mission, underline it and pray about it, asking God to help you see how
you can live up to your potential—or to help you keep going even when
you can't see how.

Option 2: The road to our full potential is filled with potential-
building choices. We can get so wrapped up in doing the big things that
we sidestep the little challenges God is using right now to prepare us.
How can you say yes to God with the little things at work? at home? at
church? Follow Moses' example and say yes.

Option 3: As you're faithful with the little challenges before you,
keep praying about the huge dreams God's put on your heart. Dream
big. If you had unlimited resources, what would you do? When you
come back to the reality of time and resources, don't throw out the big
idea. Think about small steps you can take right now toward the big
dream. If you want to start a ranch for disabled kids, start by volun-
teering at a group home. If the dream is a God-given passion, your first
steps will only stoke the fire.

Option 4: Have you ever considered your potential in the relationships you *already* have? how you could make a lasting difference as a

friend, father, brother, son, husband, or co-worker? List a few important relationships you're in and what each relationship would look like if it reached its full potential. Make time with each person to share your thoughts with him or her, and then talk together about what it would take to get there.

A MISSION THAT MATTERS

FINDING AN UNCOMMON PURPOSE AND PLAN

WHAT EACH PERSON WILL NEED:

- Bible
- Your wallet
- Pen
- Scissors

Think About It

"The dreams that God put in your heart never change. Your integrity...demands that you step up and follow those dreams to a better place, to pick yourself up yet again and push on."

COACH DUNGY

 After John 3:16, Jeremiah 29:11 is one of the most quoted Bible verses. Just as many people miss the simple truth of salvation in John 3:16, many people miss the heart of the promise in Jeremiah: " 'For I know the plans I have for you,' says the Lord. 'They are plans for good and not for disaster, to give you a future and a hope.' " Many of us forget that this promise is about *God's* plans. It doesn't say anything about *our* plans.

As we develop and think about our mission and purpose on earth, we often create our own plans then ask God to bless them. But a mission that makes a real difference, that makes the very most of our lives, comes from seeking and following God's plans. If we want a life-changing, earth-shattering mission–if we want real purpose in our lives–we need to empty ourselves of our ambition and our own plans for our lives. In exchange, God gives each of us a life of meaning, peace, and fruitfulness.

"The first step in developing a good game plan is to determine who we really are—or should be—beyond the perceptions of the world and beyond the lure of who society says we should be."

COACH DUNGY

Get in a group of four. Each of you take out one of your credit cards and throw it in the middle of the group. Then throw down your driver's license. Then toss in any membership cards you have. Now proceed to empty your wallet of its contents. If you're able, include your cash as well. (You might want to count it first.) Mix the items up a little.

As you hold your empty wallet, discuss the following questions:

▶ *What does it feel like to have all of your stuff out of your wallet?*

▶ *How easy or difficult would it be for you right now to walk away from this pile and leave the room? Why?*

▶ *How would your own ambitions and plans be affected if you walked away from everything in your pile—permanently?*

As you return the items to your wallet, carefully check to make certain you don't have something that belongs to someone else.

It's never too late to start living a mission-focused life. Who was the oldest NFL quarterback to finally accomplish his mission of winning a Super Bowl?

Talk About It

You may already have a personal mission statement. If not, you may have a vague idea of what you hope your life accomplishes. Perhaps you're just responding to life as it comes at you. None of these approaches do much good if you're not really living out what you say, hope, or think you want to be.

Imagine for a minute that you died today. For some reason, a news show found your life newsworthy and decided to do a report on you. (Or maybe it had more to do with the events surrounding your demise.) The reporter was especially smooth and endearing, so your surviving family, friends, and co-workers gave her access to your financial documents, your home, and your office. They also granted her candid and honest interviews. Take a minute or two to write down what you think—and perhaps fear—she'd find out about you (it's OK—you won't have to show what you wrote to any reporters here!):

Get back into your group from earlier and discuss the following:

▶ *What do you think the interviews would reveal about what you really care about?*

▶ *Do you think the reporter would get one fairly consistent story or a bunch of conflicting ones from the people she interviewed? Explain.*

▶ *Do you think your life matches the mission you believe God has for you? Why or why not?*

Study It

 Who answered God's question, "Whom should I send as a messenger to this people? Who will go for us?" And what answer did the person give?

 God puts passions and desires in our hearts. God created you and loves you, and wants you to enjoy and thrive in the mission he has for you. But your mission isn't really about you. Your mission is about making the most of the time God's given you for his purposes and glory. Scripture does not promise a life of ease or success. But we're given the offer of peace, meaning, and efficacy if we wholeheartedly take on the mission God has for us. Scripture gives us clear direction for our mission while on earth.

Get back into your groups, and go through each of the following Scriptures. For each of the passages, discuss the following questions:

▶ *What does this passage say about your mission?*

▶ *How would your life be different if this passage became your personal mission statement?*

1. Matthew 28:19-20

2. Micah 6:8

3. Matthew 22:36-40

4. John 4:28-29 and Hebrews 11:6

5. Proverbs 3:5-6

Afterward, discuss this question together:

▶ *What's the most difficult part of finding and following God's mission for your life?*

Live It

 Whatever your mission in life, it needs two things to line up with Scripture. First, it must be concerned with knowing and loving God. Second, it needs to include reaching out to and loving others. There are millions of approaches to living out

the mission God's given us, and we're free to take the unique approach God's put in our hearts. You don't need a complicated scheme or plan to live this mission out. You can become mission-minded and mission-focused at this very moment.

Get with a partner right now. Share what you think God is asking you to change or begin, then spend a few minutes praying for one another. When you're done, complete the card on page 51. Cut it out and put it in your wallet as a reminder to empty yourself of your own plans and pick up God's mission and plans for your life.

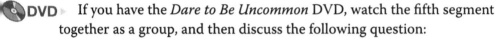 **DVD** ▶ If you have the *Dare to Be Uncommon* DVD, watch the fifth segment together as a group, and then discuss the following question:

▶ *What's your next step toward following Coach Dungy's encouragement to live a mission that matters?*

Commit to It

Before you conclude this session, commit to one or two of the action points that follow or another you come up with. Be prepared to share what happened or what you learned next week.

Option 1: Read Part VI of *Uncommon*, "Choose Influence Over Image." When you see an area where God is speaking to you, underline it and pray about it, asking God to help you see how you can make a difference in the lives or others.

Option 2: You don't need training to make a difference in someone's life. Anyone can show genuine care, concern, and love. Prayerfully consider whom God might be asking you to come alongside. Get involved in that person's life, be his friend, and wait for the opportunity to share the ideas and principles you've learned in this study. Or better yet, go and work through this study *with* him.

Option 3: Write a personal mission statement. Review the passages you just studied, and make a list of all the things that you'd like God to do through you in the lives of others. Circle one or two that really stick out to you. Then write down the people groups you have a strong desire to reach—for example the homeless, the unchurched, or young men. Circle the one that sticks out. Now put those two phrases together in a brief statement that's easy to remember. For example, "I want to bring life and freedom to the unchurched." Keep revising it until it embodies what you want your mission to be all about.

I will live out my God-given mission to the best of my abilities. I can start by:

SIGNATURE_____ DATE _____

Option 4: Don't forget that mission starts at home. Spiritual leadership begins with our families. Look over the requirements of a spiritual leader in 1 Timothy 3:1-13. Then review the passages we studied in this session with your family in mind. Make a plan for how you can be more mission-minded in your own home. Jot down your initial thoughts here:

"Love the Lord your God with all your heart, all your soul, all your strength, and all your mind...Love your neighbor as yourself."

—*Luke 10:27*

INFLUENCE OVER IMAGE

USING YOUR UNCOMMON GIFTS FOR GOD'S GLORY

WHAT EACH PERSON WILL NEED:
- Bible
- Pen

Think About It

"Being willing to be evaluated on a different scorecard is part of being an uncommon man."

COACH DUNGY

 If you've sent a child to his or her first Little League game or coached a little league team, you've seen the confusion that comes from mixed messages. Throughout the preschool years, a father orders his young son to share his toys and wait his turn. The moment the young boy steps on the basketball court, however, that same father screams, *"Steal the ball!"* After years of teaching our children to be gentle and avoid violence, we have them strap on football pads and shout, *"Hit him!"* at the kids with all our might. Fortunately, most boys catch on and learn to understand the difference between healthy competition and proper social behavior. But for many children, the first few games and practices are a little confusing.

The mixed messages don't stop after Little League. Men are constantly bombarded with opinions and ideas about what it means to be and succeed as a man. We're told that a woman *needs* a sensitive, caring, and available man, but she *wants* a strong, steely, and determined loner. The media and those around you are more than happy to tell you what you should be. But somewhere beyond the messages, ideas, and opinions is the man you really are.

Look at the list below. Designate one side of the room as "complete agreement with Message 1" and the other side of the room as "complete agreement with Message 2." As your group looks at each message, stand according to how you see yourself. For example, as you look at the category "Women," if you feel you're a sensitive and caring man, stand near the wall on that side of the room. If you're a strong and determined man, stand near the opposite wall. If you're somewhere in between, stand in the middle of the room.

If you're in a restaurant or somewhere where you can't move around the room, let each end of the table stand for the opposite messages and your cup or pen stand for you. As you go through each category, place your cup on the table according to how you see yourself.

Messages

MESSAGE 1	CATEGORY	MESSAGE 2
Women need sensitive and caring men.	Women	Women need strong and determined men.
A healthy man isn't afraid to show his emotions—including his tears.	Emotions	A healthy man is able to keep it together and always be strong.
Money is a distraction from things that are really important.	Money	You can't do the really important things if you don't have money.
A man needs other men to help him grow.	Friendship and Growth	A man needs to find his own way.
A man should find and follow his passion—no matter what the cost.	Provision	A man should provide for his family—no matter what the cost.
A man should be a "good soldier," and submit to his boss and authorities.	Work	A man should be true to himself. If others can't understand, so be it.

With a partner, discuss afterward:

▶ *How did other men's responses affect how you felt or responded during this activity?*

▶ *How is that similar to or different from how other people's opinions and messages affect your life?*

▶ *What did this exercise reveal about who you are—and how willing you are to stick to it?*

 Which NBA coach has won 1,000 games...and lost 1,000 games?

Talk About It

 Psalm 139:15-16 says that God "watched...as [you] were being formed...in the dark of the womb," and that God recorded every day of your life before you were born. God created you with complexity, he made you to be excellent, and he made you to be you. God isn't concerned with your image, what others say, or what you think you're supposed to be. He made you the way he wants you.

We all have room to grow as we are transformed into God's image, but we interrupt his plan when we try to be someone other than the person God created us to be. Imagine what

life would be like if you were able to completely tune out the outside messages of what a man's "supposed" to be. What influence could you have if you lived out the calling *God* **has on your life instead?**

Imagine that God has given you a blank page to create a description of your life—like a job description, but for every part of your life. God's only requirements are that you remain true to his Word and true to who he's created you to be. Take five minutes to jot down what your life description would look like.

_____

_____

_____

_____

_____

_____

_____

_____

_____

_____

_____

_____

_____

Share the highlights of your life description with a partner, and then discuss this question:

▶ *What would your life look like if you traded the image you want to portray, the expectations of others, and the messages you receive about yourself for the image, expectations, and message of who God created you to be?*

Study It

 Who in the Bible pretended to be crazy by scratching on doors and drooling in his beard so he wouldn't be killed by King Achish?

 For many Christian men, the problem of image isn't due to labels or expectations the world puts on us. Many Christians get caught in a different sort of image trap. We feel the pressure to appear happy when we're not, together when life is falling apart, or wise when we don't have a clue.

Worse yet, many men have perceived or imagined a pecking order in the church. We place expectations on pastors and leaders that no one can live up to–including ourselves. We put less value on less visible forms of ministry and service. If you've seen this, know that this is an image problem that Scripture *doesn't* support.

> *"You're not disqualified because of your mistakes—none of us is perfect."*
>
> COACH DUNGY

In groups of three or four, read 1 Corinthians 12:12-27 and discuss:

▶ *Describe a time when you tried to be someone or something that just wasn't you. What happened? What did you learn from it?*

▶ *Who has God made you to be? How have you seen the unique gifts and personality that God has given you displayed in the way you live?*

Have each person in your group describe which part of a human body he is most like in his God-given role in the body of Christ. For example, a person who sees himself as a quiet servant may say that he is most like a hand—he's not afraid to get dirty and nicked up as long as he gets the job done. As a group, give feedback to each person after he shares. Explain what gifts you see in him that can contribute to the body of Christ and what the body misses out on when he doesn't live that out.

Live It

 Trying to be someone we're not, portraying an image of who we want to be, or trying to meet the expectations of others always ends in frustration. We frustrate ourselves because we're either not very good at what we're doing or we're extremely unfulfilled in the work. We frustrate others because they *need* us to be doing what God created us to do.

You may not know exactly what God wants you to do, but you likely have a pretty good idea of the potential he's given you. Consider how you responded to the various messages in our Think About It activity on page 54. Take a quick look at your Life Description on page 56. And remember what part of the body you compared yourself to in our Study It time. Then complete one or two of the simple "from…to" statements that follow. In the "from" blank, list the messages, expectations, or images that you're trying to live up to that God hasn't called you to. In the "to" blank, list the role or identity that God's given you instead. One example is done for you.

I commit today to move from <u>always trying to be the smartest guy in the group</u> to <u>trying to be the most encouraging guy in the group.</u>

I commit today to move from _____

to _____

I commit today to move from _____

to _____

Share what you wrote with a partner, and then take turns praying **◄DVD**
for one another.

If you have the *Dare to Be Uncommon* DVD, watch the sixth segment together as a group, and then discuss the following question:

▶ *How can you be the person God's created you to be in the place where he's put you?*

> *"People don't care who you are or what you do; they care that you care about them."*
>
> COACH DUNGY

Commit to It

Before you conclude this session, commit to one or two of the action points that follow or another you come up with. Be prepared to share what happened or what you learned next week.

Option 1: Read Part VII of *Uncommon*, "Live Your Faith." When you see an area where God is speaking to you about how to live out your faith, underline it and pray about it.

Option 2: If you've grown because of this study, do something uncommon—start a new group that goes through this *Uncommon* study. Invite men who you believe God is calling you to reach out to. Take an interest in each person's life by checking in during the week, asking what God is doing, and spending time in prayer for each man. If you're ready for a different study, consider trying *The Driving Force* with NASCAR legend Kyle Petty.

Option 3: Sometimes we miss the opportunity to make a difference in a person's life because we're afraid of offending that person. God never calls us to be hateful or hurtful, but he does call us to be truthful. If you have a friend who's building his own prison, step up and make a difference. Ask God to give you tact and wisdom. Your friend may have a strong reaction, but if you share the truth in a loving and humble way, it's more likely that he'll be thankful for your genuine concern and care. Be honest and continue to be his friend—regardless of whether or not he takes your advice.

Option 4: Image is everywhere, and to many people image is everything. With your family, spend an evening watching TV shows you usually watch together. But before you begin watching, tell your family to look for the messages and images that each show endorses or presents. During commercials, mute the TV and discuss what you've watched. Be aware that this exercise may bring up difficult subjects, such as sexuality or substance abuse. But if your family is seeing them on TV, it's time that they start hearing about those things from *you*.

LIVE YOUR FAITH

BUILDING ON THE FOUNDATION FOR AN UNCOMMON LIFE

WHAT EACH PERSON WILL NEED:

- Bible
- Pen
- Index cards—four for each person
- Marker

Think About It

"The depth and quality of our relationship with Jesus Christ is governed by the state of our hearts. It will reveal the reasons why we do what we do."

COACH DUNGY

 Regardless of what a person believes about God, it's impossible to go through life without some measure of faith and hope. We practice faith and hope every time we drive through a traffic light–hoping and believing that the lights are working in both directions and that the other drivers are paying attention to and obeying them. People have hope for retirement investments, faith in their ability to perform at work, or hope that the future can be as good or better than the present. People have faith in science, technology, humanity, nature, and reason.

Hope and faith help us press toward the future in the midst of difficulty, make a difference in the world around us, and expect and work for change. Proverbs 13:12 tells us that "Hope deferred makes the heart sick." If we put our faith in things that can't deliver, our hopes will never be realized. Lost faith and hope lead to pointlessness, cynicism, and despair. While our investments, abilities, and reasoning may fail us, our hope in God will not disappoint us. God is worthy of our complete faith and hope, no matter what happens around us.

Give everyone four index cards.

On each card, write down one thing you put faith or hope in other than Christ. For example, you could write "My 401k" or "education" on one of your cards.

Get in groups of three or four, and share at least two of the items you wrote down. As a group, discuss how hope or faith in that thing could fail you. On the back of the index card, list some of the ideas your group discussed. For example, you could write "A 401k can quickly lose its value" or "It may be too small for what I really need in retirement."

Discuss the following questions with your group:

▶ *Is it wrong to have faith in the things your group discussed? Why or why not?*

▶ *How can the things you wrote down that you put your faith or hope in get in the way of your faith and hope in Christ?*

If there are any items that you believe you are putting *too much* faith and hope in or that God is asking you to lay down, put those cards down on the floor or table right now. Don't throw any of your cards away yet.

"Some people try to fool themselves into thinking that self-reliance is possible, but it really is foolish to think we don't have to have faith in anyone or anything else."

COACH DUNGY

Talk About It

 Hebrews 11:1 says that "faith is being sure of what we hope for and certain of what we do not see" (NIV). Faith gives us confidence that God is with us and that he's active in our lives, despite our circumstances. Hebrews 11:6 goes on to say that "it is impossible to please God without faith."

Living out our faith is much more than doing the right things, or even showing God's love to others. To live out your faith, you must have a growing and dynamic faith in Jesus. Without faith our efforts to do good, be good, or make a difference are like filthy rags (see Isaiah 64:6). But service done in and through faith makes an eternal difference for God's glory.

Faith starts with trusting Jesus and hoping in him with all our hearts. One way to grow in faith is to remember what God has done in our lives. When we see God's faithfulness in our past, we learn to trust him with our future.

With a partner, share a story about how God has come through for you in a big way. You might talk about how he saved your life, healed a relationship, or changed your heart. Then share what you've seen God do through the past six sessions as you've worked through this Bible study.

Come back together as a group and have two or three people share what their partners related. Then discuss:

▶ *What difference do you think our faith really makes to God? Explain your answer.*

▶ *What else can we do to grow in our faith, besides remembering what God's already done?*

UNcommon *Who was the youngest athlete to win a gold medal at the*
TRIVIA *Winter Olympics?*

Study It

 Coach Dungy's strength and effectiveness aren't found in his leadership prowess, his coaching brilliance, his ability to motivate, or even in his strong moral character. Tony Dungy is a man of faith. His leadership approach and his determination to do the right thing come from his faith in Jesus Christ. He's learned to trust and hope in Jesus regardless of the circumstances or outcome. God is using Coach Dungy to make a difference, both on and off the field, and Dungy is determined to make faith in Jesus the guiding force and most important aspect of his life.

Get in groups of three or four and discuss the following questions:

▶ *Read Matthew 14:22-31. Why do you think Peter's faith determined whether or not he stayed afloat?*

▶ *Read Matthew 17:20 and Matthew 21:18-22. Why is faith such an important part of living for God?*

Look once more at the titles to the first six sessions of this book. What part does faith play in living out each of these main ideas? Write your thoughts next to each title below:

1. Strengthening Your Core

2. Loving Our Families

3. Lifting Your Friends and Others

4. Your Full Potential

5. A Mission That Matters

6. Influence Over Image

 *Jesus is mentioned more times than any other man in the Bible. What two men of faith are ranked second and third by number of appearances in Scripture?*

Live It

 God has big things for you to do. He wants you to make a big difference in the lives of others around you. Just remember, God's plans are *bigger than you*. If you feel like you can accomplish God's will or effectively live out an uncommon life on your own, you're thinking too small. But with faith, anything is possible. With faith, God's purposes and plans go far beyond anything you can concoct. With faith, you can live a life that is so uncommon that it will be nothing less than remarkable.

Pick up the index cards you set on the table or floor during the Think About It section of this session. Think about what each of the cards represents in your life. For example, if you listed your 401k on your card, it may represent security or peace of mind for you.

With a marker, write a word or two that describes how faith can make a difference in each of those areas in your life. For example, you could write "God is my provider" or "security in Jesus" on the 401k card.

On a new card, write down one way you believe God is asking you to live an uncommon life. Challenge yourself to go beyond what you think you can do and list something that can only be accomplished by faith. Reflect on the lessons you've learned over the last seven weeks and consider if God has brought up recurring themes or ideas that he wants you to step out into.

Get with a partner right now. Share what you think God is saying. Then spend a few minutes praying for one another.

DVD ▸ If you have the *Dare to Be Uncommon* DVD, watch the seventh segment together as a group, and then discuss the following question:

▸ *How can you respond to Coach Dungy's challenge—to live out your faith in the way God's called you to?*

"God didn't create your life to be a series of accidents and coincidences. He knew before you were born that you would be where you are today."

COACH DUNGY

Commit to It

Before you conclude this session, commit to one or two of the action points that follow or another you come up with.

Option 1: We'll ask again: What are you doing after this study? Are you moving on to another study, or will you take the plunge and start a new *Uncommon* group with other guys who want to become uncommon men? Whatever you decide, get a plan and do it!

Option 2: The place to start an uncommon life is through a relationship with Jesus. If you or someone in your group wants a relationship with Jesus, consider walking through the following key Scriptures found in Romans:

- Romans 3:23 shows we are all sinners in need of a Savior.
- Romans 6:23 tells us that the consequence of those sins is death—eternal separation from God.
- Romans 5:8-9 says that Jesus died for our sins and frees us from condemnation.
- Romans 10:9 explains that if you "confess with your mouth that Jesus is Lord and believe in your heart that God raised him from the dead, you will be saved." Relationship with God is restored through faith in Jesus.

If *you* would like to start a relationship with Jesus, pray to him right now. Ask him to forgive you of your sins. Tell him you believe he is Lord and that you want to live your life for him. Tell your pastor or your group leader about the decision you've made to live by faith in Jesus!

Option 3: Having faith that God will take care of you is one thing—having faith that God will take care of everyone who *depends* on you is a very different matter. But living by faith means trusting in God's great love for you as well as for your family. Is fear for your family holding you back from following God with all your heart? Your obedience to God will teach your family a greater lesson. Share with your family what you believe God is calling you to do and the ways it could impact your family. Assure your family that you'll take one step at a time. Pray together, and allow your family into the process. It will build their faith and help them buy into the vision and call God's given you.

Option 4: Your time in this study will be a tremendous success if you're able to consistently live out just one principle or idea from each of the seven lessons in this book. Go back over each of the seven sessions. Try to recall the *most important* take-away you had in each session. On the next page of this book, write down that take-away in the appropriate spot. Tear the page out of the book and keep it in your Bible or someplace where you'll see it from time to time.

My take-aways:

Session 1: Strengthening Your Core

_____

_____

_____

_____

Session 2: Loving Our Families

_____

_____

_____

_____

Session 3: Lifting Your Friends and Others

_____

_____

_____

_____

Session 4: Your Full Potential

_____

_____

_____

_____

Session 5: A Mission That Matters

_____

_____

_____

_____

Session 6: Influence Over Image

_____

_____

_____

_____

Session 7: Live Your Faith

_____

_____

_____

_____

CONTACTS

Name	Phone	E-mail

CONTACTS

Name	Phone	E-mail

SESSION 1

UNCOMMON *TRIVIA*

Morgan Wootten coached high-school basketball his entire career.

UNCOMMON *EVENT*

Abraham and Isaac (see Genesis 12 and 26)

SESSION 2

UNCOMMON *TRIVIA*

Warren Moon fumbled the ball 161 times during his career.

UNCOMMON *EVENT*

Jesus asked Peter three times if the disciple loved him—the same number of times Peter denied Jesus (see John 21:15-17).

SESSION 3

UNCOMMON *TRIVIA*

Brock Huard led Seattle and his brother Damon started for Miami on November 26, 2000.

UNCOMMON *EVENT*

Abimelech (see Judges 9)

Session 4

Uncommon *Trivia*

Terry Bradshaw of the Pittsburgh Steelers threw a pass to "Frenchy" Fuqua in 1972. The pass was deflected 15 yards back to Franco Harris. Harris ran the ball in for a touchdown.

Uncommon *Event*

Miriam and her brother, Aaron, criticized Moses for marrying a Cushite. They also complained that God could speak through them just as easily as he could speak through Moses (see Numbers 12).

Session 5

Uncommon *Trivia*

John Elway led the Denver Broncos to victory in the big game when he was 37, over the Green Bay Packers—then did it again when he was 38, over the Atlanta Falcons.

Uncommon *Event*

The prophet Isaiah answered the call with the words, "Here I am. Send me" (see Isaiah 6:8).

Session 6

Uncommon *Trivia*

Lenny Wilkens. He is one of the winningest and losingest coaches in NBA history.

Uncommon *Event*

David (the future king of Israel) was hiding in Gath from King Saul. King Achish of Gath sent David away when he appeared to be crazy (see 1 Samuel 21).

UNCOMMON *TRIVIA*

Gymnast Tara Lipinski won a dramatic gold medal in 1998 when she was only 15.

UNCOMMON *EVENT*

David is mentioned 1,118 times. Moses ranks third with 740 appearances.

GOD SIGHTINGS™
LEARNING TO EXPERIENCE GOD EVERY DAY™

SEE THE BIBLE IN A NEW LIGHT...
AND EXPERIENCE GOD IN A WAY
THAT'S POWERFUL AND REAL!

With *God Sightings*, you'll discover, ponder, and embrace Bible truths—then watch for God's expression of that truth in your daily life. You and your friends will then get together face-to-face or online to share stories and compare experiences!

That's what *God Sightings* is all about—using *The One Year Bible* to look for God every day and sharing with others who are also watching for his incredible work. Soon...you'll find you can't *wait* to see what God does next.

To learn more, visit MyGodSightings.com

TYNDALE

Group

Incredible things will happen.

group.com

The ONE YEAR BIBLE